Kid Pro Quo
LITTLE PEOPLE, BIG THOUGHTS

by Lorraine Ray

Copyright © 2023 by Lorraine Ray

All rights reserved.

Danielle Estey Ray, Editor

ISBN: 9798852334640

DEDICATION

To my grandsons, Michael Jr. and Max. And to all the children I've been blessed to teach and direct. *You* are my book...

ALSO BY THIS AUTHOR:

*Yes, Cheese-us Loves Me!
Devotions for Adults,
Inspired by Kids*, 2016

FOREWORD

"Quid pro quo"—something for something. I began teaching preschool music and directing children's choirs after retiring from teaching college-level business communication. What was in it for me?

Was it lucrative? Not particularly. Did it bring me prestige? Not really. It warmed hearts, but it definitely didn't tip the scales of the esteem-o-meter. Then was it easy? Not exactly. But it felt like I was doing what I was always meant to do!

I discovered I had untapped resources stored away for "such a time as this" *(Esther 4:13)*. That was the "something" I contributed. Making music with children, watching them blossom, loving them and being loved by them, was pure joy. Plus, they made me laugh; they touched my heart; and they allowed me to be silly and spontaneous. That was the "something" I received: my *kid pro quo*.

After fourteen years in children's music, I now enjoy that same *kid pro quo* with my two inquisitive, hilarious grandsons, whose quotes are included in the final chapter of this book.

TABLE OF CONTENTS

Foreword vii
Acknowledgments xi

1 Music, Music, Music... 1
2 Faith Files 13
3 Putting the "Aww" in Awesome 23
4 Mighty Malaprops 31
5 Playful Perspectives.................................. 45
6 The M & M Chronicles................................ 71

About the Author..115

ACKNOWLEDGMENTS

Danielle Estey Ray, Editor
Michael Richard Ray, Artistic Consultant

Special friends who encourage,
support, and pray:

Lisa Fox
Judie Golden
Jamie Langston Turner
Bible Study Fellowship (BSF) friends

For the amazing opportunities:

First Presbyterian Preschool; Aiken, SC
Aiken Kinderchoir; Aiken, SC

Contributors

Cindy Alimpich
Camilla Anderson
Erinne Blackwell
Jean Covington
Cyndy Cunningham
Linda Collins
Sandra Fugate
Suzi Kilgo
Karen Kinleyside
Alysha Richardson
Karen Ross
Kathy Samaha
Steph Schneider
Joyce Teopas
Jillian Van Hefty
Rita Walker

And above all, I thank my Lord and Savior, Jesus Christ. Apart from Him, I can do nothing.

1
MUSIC, MUSIC, MUSIC...

"Music, Music, Music," a hit song from the 1950s says, "Put another nickel in, in the nickelodeon; all I need is loving you and music, music, music."

Much of the content of this chapter comes directly from my preschool music classroom or from children's choir. Highlights include convoluted song lyrics and titles, youthful insights about good singing, and—my favorite—creative excuses for not participating in music class! I also delight in the many ways my first name *(Lorraine)* is mispronounced...

❦

GIRL (age 4): Miss Er-raine, I brought my good singing voice with me today. I keep it in a special box with my toys.

After music class, three-year-old Mason couldn't wait to tell his teacher, "We SINGed a good job today!"

> *I wonder if Mason is the founder of Preschoolers Against Irregular Verbs...*

❦

And did you know that preschoolers wrote a new and improved version of "Shine, Jesus Shine"? The second stanza goes like this:

> "Flow, river flow; flood the nations with grace and MURRAY!"

> *Lord, have "murray" on me.*
> *I needed that reminder today.*

❦

A darling preschooler said she wanted to sing "Way to Go" for me, and I thought, wow, I'm not up on my pop culture 'cause I don't know that song. But...turns out I did:

> "Way to go, way to go...can't hold it back anymore...!" (from *Frozen*).

> *Way to go? Let it go? Potato, potahto.*
> *It was about a child wanting to*
> *sing her favorite song for me...*

BOY (age 3): Miss Ruh-Raine, can you "tie up" my shoes?

ME: What do you say? What's the magic word?

BOY *(proudly)*: Eighth note!

> *Captain Kangaroo, you got it wrong.*
> *The magic words aren't "please and thank you" —they're "please and eighth note."*

I had a bad case of the rainy Monday morning blahs...

ME *(to class)*: I have a new song for you today.

GIRL (age 5): I love new songs! They're like a special gift.

> *And, of course, in saying this, she gave ME a special gift...bye, bye, blahs!*

Who remembers the 1960's hit, "The Name Game"? I don't know what came over me, but I decided to teach it to my children's choir. They thought it was just about the funniest they'd ever heard. And, of course, we had to sing a chorus for everyone in the group. It was tedious but so worth the time spent...in giggles and memories. In case you've forgotten:

> Shirley, Shirley, Bo-ber-ley
> Bo-na-na fanna fo-fer-ley
> Fee-fi-mo-mer-ley
> Shirley!

The children come up with the most imaginative excuses for not participating in music class. Here are a couple of favorites:

ME *(to a preschool boy)*: Why aren't you singing today?

BOY: I have boogers in my nose.

I tried to encourage another boy's participation by reminding him he has an excellent singing voice. He gave a little grin; then responded with this: "I left my brain in bed this morning!"

Hey...you forgot me!

BOY: I can't sing. I can play instruments. I can play sports. I can't sing.

ME: Why do you think you can't sing?

BOY: I don't know how.

ME *(going way out on a limb)*: Did you know I'm a superhero? And my super power is getting kids to sing.

BOY: *(cautiously intrigued)*.

ME: *(thinking)* Now...deliver!

"Not by might, not by power, but by my Spirit."
(Zechariah 4:6). *Yeah!*

And sometimes those little ones have an innate understanding of music therapy...

KINDERGARTEN STUDENT: Once I had a bad boo-boo that really "hurted," but, when I started singing, it didn't hurt anymore!

> **"Music can heal the wounds which medicine cannot touch."**
> —Debasish Mridha

ME *(preparing three-year-olds for our upcoming program)*: We get to sing Christmas songs for our families tomorrow—are you excited?

BOY *(with great delight)*: Yeah! And my mommy says I don't have to wear nuthin'.

I asked my preschoolers to "sing out" without yelling. Because this comes up often, I decided to demonstrate how they sound when they yell. And, of course, I exaggerated. Peals of nonstop laughter ensued, followed by chants of "do it again...please...please...do it again." Then I started laughing hard, and, I don't know if I made my point at all, but the chorus of giggles was—in itself—sweet music to my ears...

How do you get three-year-olds to giggle on a Monday morning? Completely mess up the lyrics of the song you're trying to teach them! Embarrassing, but, hey...at least they're listening.

I put "Mr. Music" *(our CD player)* in time-out because he was taking too long to play our songs. The kids thought that was hilarious, and their giggles were a moment to treasure.

"A merry heart doeth good like medicine" (Proverbs 17:22, KJV).

ME *(to boy, who is often a reluctant singer)*: You really sang well today.

BOY *(smiling)*: I just got a new doctor.

I was hesitant to introduce the 1950s Perry Como hit, "Catch a Falling Star" to my preschoolers, thinking it might be too old and corny, but it passed the hardest test of all: the BOY test. A four-year-old boy made my day by asking if we could do the new "falling star" song.

*Everything old is new again...
and am I glad!*

I often sat on the edge of my table when leading children's choir. But one time, when I sat down, I forgot my keyboard was there. Plunk! I sat right on it, unwittingly inventing the Booty Boogie. Which do you think was louder—my spontaneous piano cadenza or the roars of laughter from the children?

*I have one choir member, now
in her teens, who STILL talks
about that moment...*

The music starts, and a two-year-old blurts out: "This is a BABY song!!!"

> *I hate thinking I subjected a two-year-old to singing baby songs. How insensitive of me.*

❦

ME *(to class)*: Is this an eighth note or a quarter note?

BOY: It's a quarter note. It doesn't have a flag, but it has a pole.

Get a load o' that pole!

2
FAITH FILES

This chapter highlights children's perceptions about God, religious practices, and prayer. When you ask a child to lead a prayer, you never know what you'll get! But I guarantee it will be amusing, thought-provoking, and always charming...

This one, for instance...

BOY (age 4): Music is great. Jesus is great. How did Jesus make music? Amen.

❦

BOY (age 4, *with an inevitable starter*): I pledge allegiance to the flag...

❦

GIRL (age 4): Dear God, I hope You're okay and that You have everything You need.

"Dear God: Please take my puke, so I don't puke anymore."

Isn't there a hymn that says, "Take my puke and let me be"?

GIRL (age 4): When I'm at home, I go in my room and pray in my own way. But...sometimes it makes me sad.

ME: Why does it make you sad?

GIRL: Because I'm so happy.

⚜

A girl was frantically waving her hand while we were singing "Do Lord." The stay-on-task me was sure this had nothing to do with our song or music class, but I finally gave in and called on her.

GIRL: I have a cousin who hurt his foot and had to go to the hospital and it was bad, and they had to cut it...and...um...he knows this song. 'Cause he knows every song about Gloryland!

Oh, me of little faith...

Submitted by Rita Walker of Tampa, FL:

JOSIE: When she was in seventh grade at a Christian school, her math question was, "What does 'x' equal?" She didn't actually know the answer but was quick to respond: "x equals Jesus, because Jesus is always the answer." She got half credit.

Submitted by Sandra Fugate of Knoxville, TN:

When my son was about five, he learned that Methuselah was the oldest man in the Bible. While we were out walking one day, he looked up at me and said, "Mama, are you as old as Methuselah?"

Methuselah lived to be 969 years old. I, for one, just put my dermatologist on speed dial...

I forgot to say "In Jesus' Name" at the end of our prayer in kindergarten music today but am pleased the children noticed and called me on it.

ME: I can't believe I did that!

WILLIAM *(in a reassuring tone)*: You're just confused because it's so cold.

Submitted by Erinne Blackwell of Aiken, SC:

I was reading an illustrated version of the Christmas story to my children.

VIVIAN (age 4) pointed to the shepherd and identified him as "Mary."

MOM *(gently)*: No. Remember "Mary" is the mom with the Baby Jesus.

VIVIAN *(thinking it over)*: No. Mary had a little lamb.

MOM: *Guess we still have more work to do.*

Submitted by Sandra Fugate of Knoxville, TN:

I taught a child whose last name was "Miracle." One evening when I was teaching about biblical miracles, I asked, "Do you children know what a miracle is? Young Clarence looked up and, with complete sincerity, said, "I am."

And so he is—literally and figuratively. Thank You, Lord, for the miracle of life!

We had a spontaneous little discussion about Jesus this morning in 4K music class, and I was quite impressed with their faith and knowledge.

GIRL: He loves us no matter what. He helps us when we're afraid. He's everywhere.

BOY: Yeah, even in the bathtub!!!

Good to know...

And this happened the same day as the previous "bathtub story":

ME: Who saves you?

BOY: Santa Claus.

ME: Hmm...

I soon realized, however, that those four-year-olds had varying degrees of spiritual maturity...

Submitted by Sandra Fugate of Knoxville, TN:

Six-year-old Eric was memorizing the Ten Commandments to recite in church. When his time came, he said, "Thou shalt not shove it."

Submitted by Steph Schneider of Knoxville, TN:

WILL (age 2): What's in this cup? He was referring to a communion cup at church.

MOTHER: It's Jesus' blood.

WILL *(thinking for a minute)*: Is it spicy?

You made me think, Will. "This cup is the new covenant in my blood...." (Luke 22:20). And, actually, the new covenant is "milder" than the old because it ushers in the Age of Grace. So I'm thinking that's a "no"....? I really don't know, but I surely love your question.

3
PUTTING THE "AWW" IN AWESOME

The quotes in this chapter reflect the pure and loving hearts of children:

A preschool class sang so sweetly, I told them I felt like crying, to which a girl replied, "Aww, are you missing your mommy?"

And a similar moment...

Submitted by Kathy Samaha of Aiken, SC:

KINDERGARTEN students *(to retiring preschool director)*: Why are you crying?

PRESCHOOL DIRECTOR: I'm crying because I'm leaving preschool just like you are.

JAYLONN (age 6): Ms. Kathy, are you going to first grade too?

Last week at children's choir practice, a little girl randomly blurted out:

"My mommy has one cookie left on her desk, and I'm gonna give it to you."

> *I don't need the cookie, but I'll definitely take the no-calorie sweetness behind it!*

❧

BOY (age 4, *raising his hand spontaneously*): Miss Ler-waine, I like your FOOT nails!

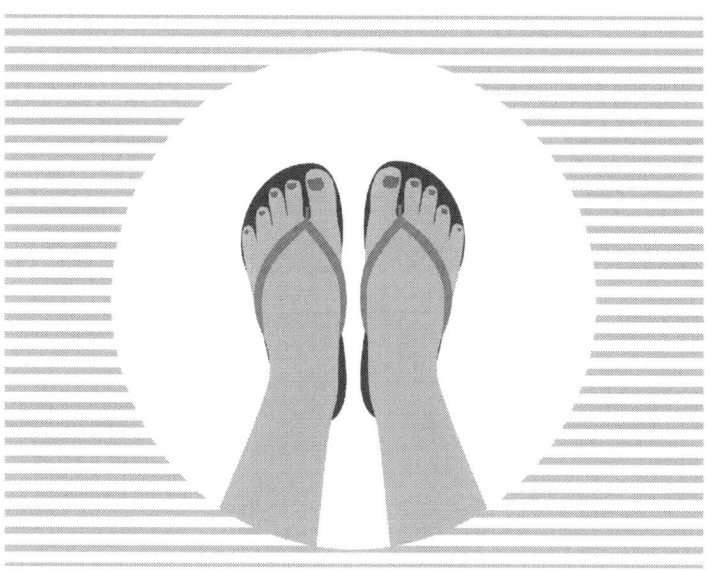

Getting your sticker in music class is a status symbol, but one girl often "passed" when offered a sparkly music note. So I gave her a hug instead of a sticker. Then the next little boy said, "I'll take a hug instead of a sticker too!"

> *A hug instead of a sticker—wow! There is so much to be learned from little ones.*

Today the children in choir were chattering about a song we all love:

GIRL: It makes me wanna cry.

BOY: I was crying in my head. My brain was raining.

Submitted by Camilla Anderson of Flagler Beach, FL:

My son Aram (age 14) wrote me a birthday card:

A birthday haiku!

That is the perfect present!

Too bad I don't have one.

A little girl was sad one morning, and I told her that music can often make people feel better. I wasn't sure if she believed me or not. Midway through class, however, she raised her hand, and, with a big smile on her face, announced, "The singing IS making me feel better!"

❦

Once upon a time, a little girl was playing with a piece of Kleenex during music class and was totally distracted; so the teacher *(moi)* finally said, "Please just get up and throw that away!" And the obedient little girl did as she was told. But, after the class left, the teacher saw that what she thought was Kleenex was actually the girl's white hair bow! And the smart little girl had not thrown it in the wastebasket. Instead she set it on a nearby table. Wow, the teacher was so embarrassed. She returned the bow, apologized to the girl, and they laughed at the misunderstanding. And they all lived happily ever after...

I was about to make an important point at Kinderchoir yesterday; that is, until I went completely blank! Said a seven-year-old boy with a young, healthy brain:

> "Don't worry, Miss Lorraine, that happens to me all the time!"

"Empathy is seeing with the eyes of another, listening with the ears of another, and feeling with the heart of another."
—Alfred Adler

Submitted by Joyce Teopas of Holland, Ohio:

Her daughter (ALISON, age 3) overheard her telling her husband the car had a dead battery. Alison slipped out of the room and soon returned, proudly holding a 9-volt household battery. "To fix your car, Mommy!"

The kindergarteners were learning a song called, "Big Dreams," so they all shared their own dreams. There were lots of dreams about playing for the national title in football, receiving awards and honors, and achieving great feats. But my favorite was from a boy who said his dream was "to just be myself."

> **"Since God made us to be originals, why stoop to be a copy?"**
> —Rev. Billy Graham

> **"To be yourself in a world that is constantly trying to make you something else is the greatest accomplishment."**
> —Ralph Waldo Emerson

4
MIGHTY MALAPROPS

Malapropism (as defined by Oxford): "the mistaken use of a word in place of a similar-sounding one, often with an unintentionally amusing effect, as in, 'dance a flamingo' (instead of *flamenco*)."

Writers of sitcoms know how to use malapropisms to their fullest advantage. For example:

(1) Said Archie Bunker on *All in the Family* when ordering at an Italian restaurant: "I'll have the *veal scallopeepee!*"

(2) Said Jennifer on *Family Ties* about her seventeen-year-old crush: "He can't help it—he's got *Mormons* coursing through his veins!"

Of course, those lines were deliberately written that way for comedic effect. When children do it, however, their innocence makes their little flubs endearing and often hilarious.

CHILDREN'S CHOIR MEMBER: When I sang my solo, I got lots of "condiments."

Hold the mayo, please...

"Everyone likes a compliment."
—Abraham Lincoln

"I can live for two months on a good compliment."
—Mark Twain

Not exactly a malapropism, but a fun analysis of words: We were singing "Catch a Falling Star." I asked the preschoolers if they knew what "multiplying" was because it was in the lyrics. One child proudly exclaimed, "It's when you MULT."

What can I say? This child understands how words are formed! But just how does one "mult"?

❦

Same song as in the previous story. The line in question is, "So when your troubles start multiplying, and they just might…" Another student thought we were saying multi-FLY.

I get it. When little ones leave doors open in the summer, it often leads to a multi-fly situation!

BOY (age 4): Miss Ruhlaine, look at my sore. It's INFESTED.

Ewww. Hopefully not with those darn multi-flies...

Submitted by Alysha Richardson of Aiken, SC:

MALLORY (age 7): Logan, stop it! If you don't, I'm going to tell Mom you're being an "**A** Double **Ass**."

So much for spelling to avoid saying the naughty word...

GIRL (age 5): How will anyone hear my solo? I don't have a MICROSCOPE.

Submitted by Suzi Kilgo of Aiken, SC:

The family was headed for a trip to Florida, and two-year-old Caroline kept hearing them talk about *Miami*.

CAROLINE: Mommy, what is "your ami"?

You can't beat the humor and charm of children's misconstrued song lyrics!

The actual lyrics: "Give me that old time RELIGION…"

Sung by CHILD: "Give me that old time PIGEON…"

Actual lyrics: "And God sent our *salvation* this blessed Christmas morn..."

Sung by CHILD: "And God sent our SALIVATION..."

And song titles too...

Actual title: "Go Tell it on the Mountain"

Child's title: "Old Yeller on the Mountain"

Actual Lyrics: "Now bring us some figgy pudding..."

Child's Lyrics: "Now bring us some FREAKIN' pudding..."

⚜

ME: Who wants to choose our last song today?

GIRL (age 3): Could we do "Ho Ho Santa"?

ME: I don't think I know it. Will you sing it for me?

GIRL: *(doing all the hand gestures)*

ME: Ohhh...I think you mean, "HO-HO-HO-HOSANNA."

GIRL: *(smiling and nodding her head)*

Submitted by Alysha Richardson of Aiken, SC:

LOGAN (age 7): Mom, can we use the Cherokee?

MOM: What is that?

LOGAN: the Cherokee Machine.

MOM: I don't know what that is, Baby. Can you tell me more?

LOGAN: *(Starts singing a familiar tune)*

MOM: Ohhh....KARAOKE.

Submitted by Karen Ross of Columbus, OH:

Though we'd driven to Florida before, we were considering flying this time. After all, there wasn't much to see except Atlanta and its many-storied buildings.

MACEY (age 5, *echoing their thoughts*): Yeah, it's just Aunt Linda and the pie-scrapers.

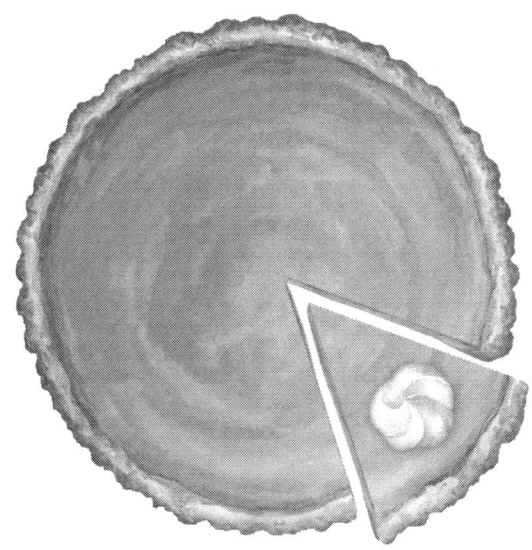

ME *(to children's choir)*: We're going to Anchor Rehab to sing for the RESIDENTS.

GIRL *(with great exuberance)*: We're gonna sing for the PRESIDENT?!

5
PLAYFUL PERSPECTIVES

How do you keep four-year-olds in stitches? Completely lose your voice in the middle of a song!

So, why hire a clown for your next children's party? I'm available...

> *Sometimes it's worth being the butt*
> *of a joke to hear little ones giggle.*
> *Is there a more beautiful sound?*

Submitted by Jean Covington of Aiken, SC:

MADDUX (age 6, *when his Mimi opened an invitation to a baby shower*): Why would anyone want to watch a baby take a shower?

You have a point, Maddux!

A girl in Kinderchoir told us how a "laughter outbreak" infected a whole school in Japan, including the teachers. It went on so long and was so widespread that, supposedly, they even dismissed school that day. So we started imagining what it was like—and, of course, we laughed… and laughed…and laughed…every one of us…for a VERY long time!!!

Submitted by Cindy Alimpich of Aiken, SC:

Landon (age 4) loved watching NASCAR with his dad. Because they often went to the bathroom together, they had a special "potty ritual" for this event. As they prepared to "go," they would say in unison: "Gentlemen, start your engines!"

BOY (age 7, *offering a football tip*): Don't root for the Patriots 'cause New England was mean to the United States!

*Everything I know about history,
I learned in children's choir.*

❦

One day in preschool music, hands were flying up every two seconds. Everyone wanted to share something.

ME: I'd love to hear what y'all have to say, but we'd use up our time, and I'm here to teach you music. That's my job!

BOY *(spontaneously)*: Yeah...and, if you don't do it, you'll get fired!!!

❦

ME: I need you to do the hand gestures that go with our song.

BOY (age 4): I'm too tired.

ME: Then you might be too tired to get your sticker!

BOY: Oh, I'm not that "too tired"!

Submitted by Linda DelFrate Collins of Mansfield, OH:

You know you're in trouble when your not-quite-three-year-old granddaughter, Josie, has exhausted all excuses for not taking a nap and comes up with this:

"Hey, I'm crying real tears here!"

At times, we all need *(ahem)* constructive feedback...

I was coming out of the restroom stall, and a four-year-old girl was waiting to go in. I gave her a big smile and said, "Here ya go."

GIRL *(very annoyed)*: You use too much toilet paper.

I guess I've been warned.

❦

ME: Your haircut is so pretty and grown-up.

GIRL (age 7): Well, if I'm going to ring jingle bells for our choir program, I have to look professional.

❦

At last, I can stop tossing and turning at night, wondering why something feels different...

KERI (age 3, *barely containing her excitement*): Miss Luh-waine, I have a big suh-pwise faw you. 'Member how last year my favorite color was "puhple"?

ME: *(nodding, pretending to remember)*

KERI: Well, now it's pink!!!

ME *(to neighbor girl)*: Oh, what a pretty cat! What's its name?

GIRL: He's pregnant right now.

ME: Oh, I see, but what's her name?

GIRL: He's just pregnant.

Well, I concede. It's a tomcat, and his name is "Pregnant Right Now" or "Just Pregnant," for short...

Today a little boy sneezed, so I gave him a tissue. Within seconds, almost everyone in the class was "sneezing." Having spent most of my professional life teaching college, I never realized Kleenex was such a hot commodity among preschoolers.

When one of your older choir members (age 8) says, "I'm getting to that age where I don't like to stand up..."

Girl, if you're feeling that way now...just wait a few decades!

One summer when I taught music for Vacation Bible School:

GIRL (age 5, *with great surprise*): You're the same "Miss Meraine" that's in our music class!

ME: Why, yes, I am!

I just wave my wand and magically appear wherever children are singing.

BOY *(after I asked him to focus)*: Miss Lorraine, I had three pieces of pumpkin pie with whipped cream, and I'm completely cuckoo. But then I'm ALWAYS a little cuckoo!!

Gotta love a guy who knows himself!

"Knowing your weaknesses is a strength, not a weakness."
—Kim Harrison

I was concerned that my younger singers might not understand the word *occupation*, which was mentioned in our song. I asked if anyone knew what it meant.

GIRL: It's like...when you have nothing else to do... your occupation fills up your time and keeps you from getting bored.

"Find a job you love, and you will never have to work a day in your life."
—Mark Twain

Submitted by Erinne Blackwell of Aiken, SC:

This is what I overheard during tonight's bedtime story, THE HOBBIT:

DAD: Bilbo's heart jumped into his mouth.

James (age 6): Eeeewwwww!

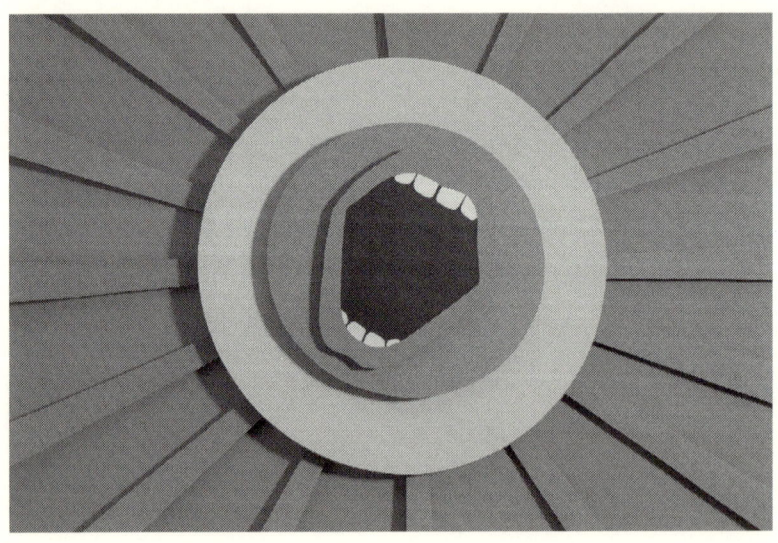

I love how kids are so literal!

One of our vacation Bible school songs was called, "No One Like You," so the title appeared on our projector. A boy pointing to the screen, asked, "Miss Lorraine, why does it say, "No One Likes You"?

Ah, the difference just one letter can make!

❦

This is so "last century," but, in the "olden days" when I taught high school typing on actual typewriters, we had to make corrections with an eraser. This was even before correction tape and correction fluid came on the scene. When students turned in an assignment, they were marked down if their corrections were not made neatly. So I gave them this tip that always helped me: If the paper gets a little smudgy or discolored from erasing, try using a bit of chalk on the paper to brighten it. That day, a student turned in a business letter that was covered with yellow dots...

What can I say? She did just what she was told. It never occurred to me to specify white chalk only...

My 4K music class decided to teach me to floss. My first attempt brought about peals of giggles followed by: "No, Miss Lorraine, that's not flossing—that's the twist!!"

Hey, I could do a mean twist back in the day! Let's just call it

Flossing: AARP Style

I had a serious talk with my preschoolers about what they could do differently so they could all earn their music stickers. There were many insightful responses, but I have to say…my favorite was, "Next time I'm going to bring my enchanted voice."

Submitted by Cyndy Cunningham of Toledo, OH:

When my daughter Kim was three years old, I decided to have my hair cut. When I showed her the new look, this was her reaction:

KIM: *(staring, then crinkling up her nose)*: Put it BACK!!!!

Submitted by Karen Kinleyside of Dayton, OH:

We were watching a cattle show at a county fair in KY when five-year-old Andrea said loudly while examining a steer, "What is that down there?" I was scrambling trying to think how to explain about his male parts. There was silence, as everyone seemed to be waiting to see what the veterinarian's wife was going to come up with. I said, "Well, that's where he goes pee."

ANDREA: Oh, I know that! But what's that ball at the end of his tail?

"Everything is both simpler than we can imagine, and more complicated than we can conceive." —Goethe

Submitted by Karen Ross of Columbus, OH:

Eleven-year-old Macey had just taken the biscuit she made for a 4H competition out of the oven. Her mom, standing nearby, shook her head.

MOM: That biscuit sure won't win any prizes. You're not going to enter it, are you?

MACEY: Yes. I am. I might earn some points.

So that afternoon she took her pitiful-looking biscuit to be judged. The result? A blue first-place ribbon for Macey! Okay, so it was the only entry. But this meant she could advance to the regional competition. And, for regional, her mom bought fresh ingredients. And the resulting golden, flakey biscuit brought a second-place ribbon for Macey.

"If you don't give up on something you truly believe in, you will find a way."
—Roy T. Bennett

Macey found a way, and she was a winner!

In church, I received a dandelion, which was more beautiful than a dozen roses, because it came from a sweet little girl saying, "Miss Lorraine, I have a surprise for you!"

ME: You totally made my day!

GIRL: Yeah, I know.

Submitted by Jillian Van Hefty of Bella Vista, AK:

My son, Alex, then five years old, filled in the blanks for this special book for DAD:

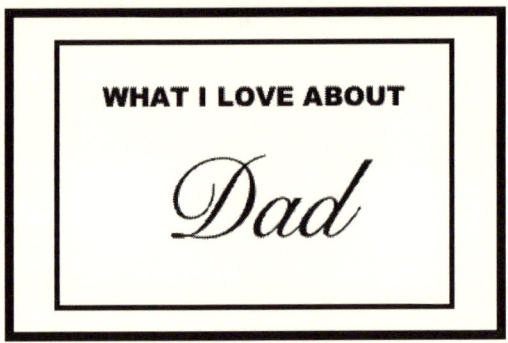

Here is his response to No. 47:

I don't know what I'd do without ~~your~~
_____mom_____.

What I like best about Dad is...Mom?

And this one...from her other son, Charlie (age 4):

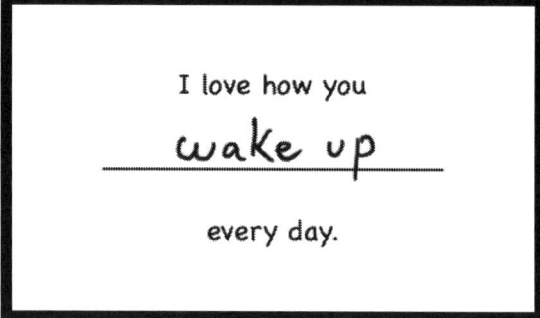

"90 percent of parenting is just thinking about when you can lie down again."
—Good Housekeeping

Submitted by Alysha Richardson of Aiken, SC:

ME *(to both children)*: Grab the mail and trash can, please.

MALLORY (age 7): It's my turn to roll the trash can back.

MOM: It's dark, so let Logan (older brother) pull it away from the road a bit first.

MALLORY *(to Logan)*: Ya know what that means, don't you? Mom, doesn't care if *you* get hit by a car!

⚘

Submitted by Camilla Anderson of Flagler Beach, FL:

DAD: There was a giant earthquake on Mars this week.

ARAM (age 7): Dad, there can't be an earthquake on Mars—there can only be a MARSquake!

Submitted by Rita Walker of Tampa, FL:

DREW (age 6) was doing story problems in math.

TEACHER: Show how you got your answer.

So he drew a picture of his head with an arrow going in one side and exiting the other.

DREW: I thought about it.

Submitted by Alysha Richardson of Aiken, SC:

Four-year-old Mallory was sitting on the porch steps watching kids play in the yard. She walked up to me and looked intently at the top of my head.

MALLORY: Oh, Mommy, I love your sparkly hairs!

Puzzled, it took me a minute to realize she was talking about my grays!

"A gray head is a crown of glory;
It is found in the way of righteousness"
(Proverbs 16:31)

6

THE M & M CHRONICLES

Meet my grandsons, the M & M's. The oldest one is Michael Jr. *(also known MJ, Minky, or Mink)*; the younger one is Maximus *(Max or Maxxy)*. These little guys have enriched my life in countless ways, one of which is providing rich jewels to add to my treasure chest of kid quotes.

Part I: In Sync with "Mink"

When he was about seven months old, he became fascinated with "This Little Piggy." He especially liked when I demonstrated with my own toes, so he could watch carefully. He would get so excited for the "whee, whee, whee" part that, after the third toe, he couldn't hold back and beat me to the punch, shrieking "whee, whee, whee" all the way home…

I can relate to this. Even after my dream trip to Hawaii, my favorite place to be is "all the way home." I was shouting "whee, whee, whee" too. Spiritually, when I get overly bogged down with everyday concerns, I'm reminded to focus on my eternal home. And…what brought "Dorothy" back to Kansas? A magic wand and, "There's no place like home; there's no place like home; there's no place like…"

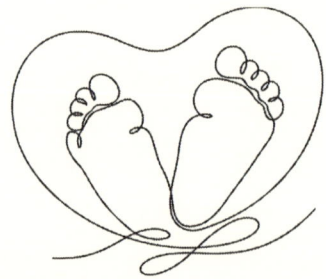

ME: What does a lion say?

MINKY (age 17 months, *proudly*): Please!!!!

Gotta love a polite lion!

When he asked for lunch, I thought he might like something a bit different. I heated up what I thought was a yummy burrito and cut it up in small pieces. He was 21 months old at the time.

MINKY *(a bit peeved)*: No! Not "dis"! LUNCH!!!!

❦

When he was two, I gave him a pair of joggers for Christmas, and he called them his "comfy pants."

> *I guess the nonstop corporate*
> *attire gets old...*

❦

After helping him brush his teeth before bedtime, he looked up at me with the utmost sincerity and declared, "You're doing so well."

A little role reversal here? Hey, Minky, I'm the one who's supposed to tell YOU you're doing well. But, hey, I'll take it...the ability to affirm others is a beautiful trait.

❦

I often call him "Sweet Cakes." One night I put him to bed, and, before I closed the door, I heard his little voice say to me: "'Night, Sweet Cakes"...

MINKY (age 2, *when his walking advanced to running*): I'm fasting!

You mean...I can fast without giving up food? 'Love that concept!

How quickly Christmas can become addicting! The day after Christmas, Mommy and Daddy came home with grocery bags,

MINKY (age 2, *screaming with delight*): Presents!

My first text from MINKY (age 2): Cc.;:490$!$89

I ask you: does anything say love like Cc;:490$!89?

He frequently anticipates and mimics what adults are apt to say, so, after asking for a third helping of his favorite cheese...

MINKY (age 2 1/2): Goodness gracious, my man!!!

And I surely would have said that... or something quite similar. Spot on!

❦

ME: *(saying "good night" and closing the door)*: I love you!

MINKY *(after door closed)*: SO MUCH

❦

MINKY: Hi LoLo—with your perfect head and blue eyes—and BIG EARS!

Doh! It started out so well. Then my bubble burst, and all I could think of is, "Grandmother, what big ears you have!"

MINKY (age 3): Once upon a time LoLo came to see me, and she brought me muffins, and she went pee-pee all by herself!

I'm so glad he noticed. I've been working hard at it...

❀

I was trying everything to ease three-year-old Minky out of a meltdown—distracting him, trying to make him laugh, starting to read to him—all things that usually work. But this time, he just stated emphatically, "NO, LoLo. I just have to cry!"

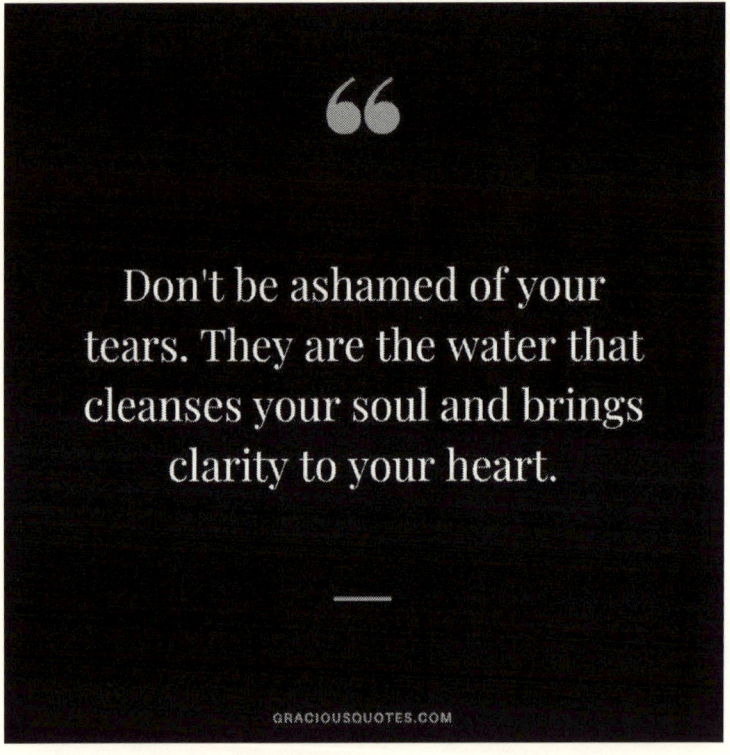

*I needed that reminder.
Go ahead and cry, Little Man...*

MINKY *(when naked)*: I can't go out. I'm in my penis!

***

There was a kind couple who lived across the street from Minky. Their names were "Buck and Suzy." What Minky heard, however, was "Bucken Suzy." And sometimes he would ask for a special "guy visit" with Bucken...

***

MINKY (age 3) paid me a compliment—sort of. When learning I was coming to visit him, his response was: "LoLo...there is no better guy than that!"

> *I'm good with being a "guy," as long as*
> *I'm a good guy in your eyes, Minky!*

***

He was four when I started teaching him how to play Bingo. When he heard that certain number he'd been waiting for, he exclaimed, "I've been waiting for this one for years and years and years!"

***

MINKY (age 4 ½) had a bad case of the hiccups.

ME: My grandpa—your great-great grandfather—taught me the best way to get rid of hiccups. It never fails. Put your pinkies in your ears. I'll hold a glass of water; then you take a sip.

MINKY *(listening with great interest; then, after thinking it over...)*: Or...I could just wait for the hiccups to go away.

⚘

We were playing a game with state capitals.

MINKY (age 4 ½): Well, I know Salt Lake City is the capital of U-HAUL...

MINKY: And now I'm going to give you a kiss 'cause you did such a good job on your hugs!

I like the way you think, Mink!

ME: I'm so glad to see you.

MINKY: Me too. You're always on my brain.

❦

MINKY: Oh, I know who God is. He was in "Fiddler on the Roof."

Yes, He certainly was!

❦

When I suggested to the boys that we play and sing, "Itsy Bitsy Spider"…

MINKY: Oh yeah! But our favorite song is actually "Separate Ways" by Journey.

*So much for children's music…
they're way too cool for me!*

❦

ME *(via telephone conversation)*: It's only been a week since I've seen you, but you sound so grown up.

MINKY (age 4): Yeah, my voice is still pretty high though!

❦

A science lesson...

ME: What are you eating?

MINKY: A biscuit. You see...the biscuit turns to energy and then comes out later as poop and pee.

❦

MINKY (age 5): wanted me to play a game with him, and I said I would as soon as I finished *conversing* with Mom and Dad.

Later that same day...

ME: Okay, I can play Zingo with you now, Minky.

MINKY *(a bit weary)*: Why were you *consequencing* so long?

❦

He was proudly sharing what he learned from his then-favorite book, HOW THINGS WORK.

MINKY: Lye is a chemical made from the "asses" of burnt wood.

❦

Together, Minky and I read the book, STRICTLY NO ELEPHANTS, by Lisa Mantchev. We loved how the boy carried his pet elephant over cracks in the sidewalk. A few hours later, I complimented him for being helpful, and he remembered the message of the book:

MINKY: That's what friends do. They help us over the cracks.

> **"Oh, I get by with a little help from my friends!"**
> —John Lennon and Paul McCartney

He was watching and interacting with a Little Einstein video called, "A Galactic Good-night."

VOICE ON VIDEO: What do *you* do before going to bed?

MINKY: Well, I usually pee.

ME *(in a conversation with Minky's dad)*: I'm not sure. I'm really torn.

MINKY *(horrified)*: LoLo's torn???

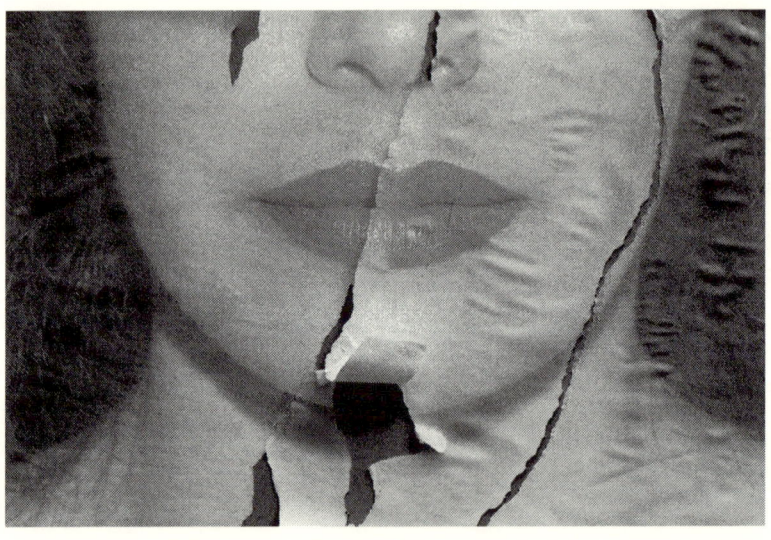

MINKY (age 6): If sugar isn't healthy, why was it even invented? I'm so attracted to it..."

Why ARE we attracted to that which isn't good for us? An age-old question. Back in the Garden of Eden, Adam and Eve had so many trees from which they could eat. Why were they attracted to the one tree that was forbidden? And we've all been struggling ever since...

"There is a charm about a forbidden fruit that makes it unspeakably desirable."
—Mark Twain

"While forbidden fruit is said to taste sweeter, it usually spoils faster."
—Abigail Van Buren

He saw and heard windchimes on the front porch.

MINKY: The wind makes them play, so I'll call them "wind-struments."

Makes perfect sense to me...

❦

Speaking of "wind" instruments...

MINKY *(to his mom)*: Mommy, I know what the F-word is.

He then whispers in her ear: FART.

*Oh, let that innocence last
as long as possible!*

❦

MINKY *(to Mom and Dad)*: I haven't got much elbow grease, but I can write some cursive.

MOM AND DAD *(giggling)*: What?

MINKY: Elbow grease is a real thing, you know. It helps you write in cursive and stuff.

❦

MINKY *(to Dad)*: Max is with me at the doctor for "mortal" support. Right, Dad?

❦

MINKY: My brother's name is "Maximus" like *gluteus maximus*, which means BUTT.

❦

MINKY *(to me)*: LoLo, when the wind blows, your hair looks like lobster tentacles!

Not exactly the look I was going for—but love the imagery...

MINKY *(idly singing "Que sera sera")*:
... 🎵 Whatever will be, will be; the future's not ours to SMASH... 🎵

❦

MINKY: LoLo, I really like your car, but maybe you could add some images.

ME: Like what?

MINKY: Like purple dots.

MAX (age 4): Or "billains" *(villains)*.

MINKY: Or bologna sandwiches!

Clearly, I'm not thinking outside the box!

MINKY: I love "Alexa" because she can answer all of my questions.

But can she make your favorite food or tickle you?

❦

I spilled some vanilla extract, and Minky couldn't resist putting his hands in it.

ME: Why did you put your hands in that?

MINKY: Um...I thought it was hand sanitizer.

MINKY *(to me)*: You're Dad's mom, so Mother's Day still means something to you, right?

❦

DAD *(to MAX)*: You've got syrup on your fingers, and I'm wearing my good jeans!

MINKY: He *does* love those jeans!

❦

ME *(to Minky after he learned to use the Keurig coffeemaker)*: This coffee is especially good.

MINKY: Because I made it, it's extra sweet, right?

❦

MINKY: I like to relieve my stress by watching satisfying Tetris videos.

❦

MINKY *(at the dinner table)*: The macaroni part of my stomach is 99 percent full, but the applesauce part still has available space.

MINKY *(when brother Max was having difficulty finding his underwear in his backpack)*: If it smells like *butt*, it's underwear!

Minky and I were talking about major and minor chords. When I played the major chord, this was his response:

"That chord sounds like someone just got a great idea!"

MINKY *(looking in my refrigerator)*: I like that there's a whole shelf just for Diet Coke!

Busted.

❦

We were using flashcards for a rhyming exercise and came to the word love.

MINKY: Oh, *love*. Like what you and I have…

Aww….

Part 2: Blessed to the "Max"

ME: Say you're sorry to Minky.

MAX: (age 2, *with a big toothy smile*): But "I not"!

My point was lost but gotta love the honesty!

❀

We had pizza on paper plates for Max's second birthday party, and he loved it.

MAX: More "plate-za," please…

Why use two words when one does the job? I knew exactly what he meant…

❀

ME *(correcting Max when he said something unkind)*: Say nice things to your brother.

MAX (age 3, *proudly and obediently*): Nice things to your brother!

Why did I expect anything else?

❀

I was talking to the boys on the phone—apparently this is a lost art for the screen kids of the Alpha generation...

MINKY: Max, wanna say "hi" to LoLo?

MAX: Hi LoLo. Something's wrong—I can't SEE you!

MAX *(after dropping a piece of his pancake on the floor)*: Ooops, I forgot all about my mouth!!!

Once upon a time, Max (age 3) was engrossed in playing his favorite songs on my phone. But, all of a sudden, disaster struck...

MAX *(urgently)*: I wanna play Mama...can't find "Mama, Mama, Ooh."

I was dumbstruck for a second. Then it occurred to me: He wanted to hear "Bohemian Rhapsody." So glad those Queen lyrics came back to me—whew! Peace and harmony restored...

Max reminded me of a spiritual truth. In his four-year-old consciousness, "not now" meant "no" and, therefore, was cause for a meltdown; for example, "You *never* let me watch that...*(with pouty lower lip).*" I think sometimes I'M like that when an answer to prayer seems to be "not now" instead of the desired "yes." Why is waiting so infuriating? I think there is still a toddler lurking in all of our hearts. I put myself in "time out" to reflect on this and have decided to recommit to trusting God's perfect timing.

I asked Max to turn his inside-out shirt the right way. Interestingly, this happened at the end of summer when people were talking about getting back to the routine, going back to school, and the like...

MAX: I just don't want to get back to normal yet!

❦

MAX (age 4, *looking so charming in his black and white striped shirt*): LoLo, I'm wearing stripes like "roberts" wear.

ME: Who's Robert?

HIS MOM *(translating for me)*: not the name Robert—the guys that get put in jail for stealing: ROBERTS.

> *And there's nothing like a good game of cops and "roberts"...*

MAX *(looking at a card on my countertop)*: Who's that from?

ME: Missy.

MAX: Where does she live?

ME: Michigan

MAX (age 4): Oh Michigan...where there's NO SHARKS!

Who cares about those harsh Michigan winters when you could be avoiding sharks?

MAX *(seeing this bag hanging from my doorknob)*: LoLo, I didn't know you got a cheetah!!!

MAX *(wondrously, as he looked at a photo of his father in a dark-colored coat)*: Is my daddy a policeman?

He may not be a policeman, but he certainly looks out for those boys of his!

"Dad is, and always will be, my living, breathing superhero."
—Bindi Irwin

I had been idly singing "Tradition," and MAX said, "That's RIDDLER on the Roof." We both got excited and ended up watching the film together, but I had a hard time convincing him that "Lazar Wolf" isn't actually an animal...

AH-ooooooo!

MAX *(to his mother at bedtime)*: But, Mommy, my feet aren't under the "cuddlers"...

I'm with you, Max. I like my feet under the cuddlers too...

MAX (age 5, *when he's had enough to eat*): My tummy's getting stressed out...

WARNING: This story is blush-worthy. Read if you dare...

I left the door open when I used the bathroom, so I could Toilet Supervise the grandkids...

MAX (age 4, *pausing outside the bathroom*): LoLo, I saw your tush, but I didn't see your "china."

Whew! That's a relief. Only the china-cologist needs to see that...

MAX: I'd like to watch "The Gingerbread Man" movie.

ME: How about we do that right before you go to bed? You can get your pajamas on, brush your teeth, and then we'll watch it.

MAX: *(patting my head rhythmically)*: Why...that. would. be. LOVELY!

❀

MAX (age 4) was beginning to grasp his family relationships. Once, when his dad was backing out of my driveway, he called out the car window, "Bye, Daddy's mommy!"

❀

MAX: LoLo, how's your day going? Can I watch this video on YouTube? It's not "biolent."

Besides chuckling over the word "biolent," I was amused that he began his request with a moment of friendly chit-chat. He's learning the art of "winning friends and influencing people"...and it worked. I said "yes"...

❀

Max noticed a photo of me on the wall. It was actually fairly recent, but he exclaimed, "That's you, LoLo. You were just a baby!"

He was listening to a brand-new song, which had his full attention. When the bridge of the song began, he uttered, "Ooh...it's getting classical, Dude."

❦

He beat me at Candyland. His reaction: "LoLo, you forgot to win!"

> *Hmm. I think my football team "forgot" to win too!*

❦

Sometime those little guys will say something that is technically naughty *(potty language)*, but it's genuinely funny. One particular time, I had a hard time keeping a straight face.

MINKY: LoLo, are you trying not to laugh?

MAX: She's laughin'!

ME: *I completely lost it.*

> **"A day without laughter is a day wasted."**
> —Charlie Chaplin

MAX *(to his teacher when he fell down)*: Why weren't you looking where I was going?

❀

ME *(when I spilled something in the kitchen)*: Oh… yucky poo!

MAX: You can't say "poo," LoLo. That's potty talk.

❀

MAX (age 5) was outside playing and told me he was hungry. I gave him a little plastic bag containing pretzel chips, and he was delighted:

> "That was just what I was wanting—
> an outdoor family snack!"

> *Sometimes the littlest things delight children…I have to ask myself if I'm remembering to fully enjoy the small pleasures of life.*

❀

MAX (age 5): Once upon a time there were three bears, and they lived happily ever after. Then Goldilocks came.

Yeah, that Goldilocks ruined everything.

❦

And speaking of fairy tales...

MAX: I want to read Hansel and PRETZEL.

MAX: Here ya go, Grandma—I mean, LoLo.

ME: Well, I'm still your grandma—I just go by "LoLo."

MAX: Then I should call you "Lo-ma."

ME: Ask Alexa to play Beethoven's Fifth.

Max: Alexa, play Beethoven SMITH.

> *I love listening to the music of great composers like Johannes Sebastian Bach, Wolfgang Amadeus Mozart, and Beethoven Smith.*

❦

ME: Boys, I'm not gonna be happy if this Easter egg dye ends up on my rug.

MAX: Don't worry, LoLo; if it spills, Super Max is here to clean it up for you!

MAX *(when he opened the box containing his Hulk pajamas)*: This is my best life in the whole wide world!

"Find gratitude in the little things, and your well of gratitude will never run dry."
—Antonio Montoya

Max was just a little excited when he received a bobble head of Bruce Banner/Hulk.

"When's your birthday, LoLo? 'Cause I'm going to get you one just like it!"

**"When you learn, teach.
When you get, give."**
—Maya Angelou

And the Hulk again...

MAX *(to me)*: If any monsters come, you send them to me. I'll turn into the Hulk and defeat them! But you'll have to wear a costume...

Hey, if it means I'm safe from monsters, I'm good with that costume!

MAX *(coming to Mom and Dad with cupped hands)*: Here, I lost my tooth.

MOM *(concerned)*: I didn't know it was loose.

MAX *(shrugs)*.

MOM *(somewhat alarmed)*: Did you force it to come out? That must have hurt. Why?

MAX *(staunchly)*: I wanted the money.

The two boys and I were decorating Minky's birthday cake. I was enjoying myself thoroughly—that is, until my body language came under scrutiny...

MAX: Why are your arms like that? People have their arms like that when they're about to throw a fit!

For years, I sang "Where is Thumbkin?" with my preschoolers. When I sang the "Hear, I am..." part, I used a silly voice to suggest it was really another person singing. The students giggled, and it was a sweet moment. Well...I tried that on Max, and this was his reaction:

> *"Don't sing in that scratchy voice. It sounds like an old man. Sing it right."*

❧

ME *(to Max)*: If I let you stay up too late and you're grumpy tomorrow, it will be my fault!

MAX: Yeah, you might even get arrested!

The boys discovered my Apple watch and all the fun things it could do. I told them it was primarily a safety device for me, since I live alone. MAX *(the empath)*: You *don't* live alone, LoLo, 'cause I'm gonna come visit you at your house every day.

ABOUT THE AUTHOR

Lorraine Ray lives in Knoxville, Tennessee, and is an associate professor *emeritus* at Ohio University. She has also been a preschool music teacher and is the founder-director of Aiken Kinderchoir.

Much of her writing is humorous and often revolves around her faith. Her short plays have been performed at South Carolina writers' conferences. And, in 2005, she was the winner of the Carrie McCray Literary Award for nonfiction.

Her devotional book, *Yes, Cheese-us Loves Me!* was published in 2016. And she was one of 40 women whose essays were selected for the humor anthology, *Laugh Out Loud*, by Allia Zobel Nolan. In 2018, Lorraine was the winner of *The Saturday Evening Post* limerick contest.

Please visit Lorraine at www.lorraineray.com and "like" *KID PRO QUO* at https://www.facebook.com/profile.php?id=61552571215733

Made in the USA
Columbia, SC
29 November 2023

39bc2c26-c1a1-4617-a723-729f03488392R01